The Influence Zone:

Leadership Intelligence That Ignites Results

30 Days of Impact
30 Learning Lessons
30 Reflection Activities

Doreen M. Lecheler

Doreen M. Lecheler
THE INFLUENCE ZONE:
Leadership Intelligence that Ignites Results

Authored by: Doreen Lecheler

Published by: VisionLinked, Inc.

Text and Cover Design by: Megan Wilbur

Cover Graphics by: Nic Lecheler

ISBN-13: 978-1-7336902-2-5

Printed and bound in the United States of America

INTRODUCTION

Creating & Maintaining Meaningful Change

Do you consciously consider how your interactions with others will affect them or whether your behavior will help facilitate mutually beneficial outcomes in your sphere of influence? Most people don't. They tend to act or respond in the moment with subconscious impulses and attitudes.

If you're not consciously choosing your words, actions, and attitudes with thoughtful intent then you're likely acting from spontaneous habit and careless neglect. The choices you make determine the maximum radius of your impact, otherwise known as your Influence Zone. To achieve inspirational motivation, cooperation, and optimum effect, you must connect in ways that engage others toward mutually rewarding, purpose-driven outcomes.

This is the essence of leadership intelligence. Thanks to unveiling research in the neurocognitive sciences, we now know that intelligence has many more facets than the age-old IQ test. Leadership success requires a wide range of talents that manifest through multiple skills.

Of course, leadership requires strategic, tactical and analytical talents, but emotional intelligence and social intelligence play an equally, if not greater, impact on the success of your influence on others.

Emotional intelligence, or intrapersonal intelligence, is the degree to which you are aware of your own life experiences and how those stored thoughts and emotions are triggered, interpreted and managed in your current situations. In other words, when experiences cause you to feel anger, frustration, worry, fear, or more, does past emotional memory hijack your new experience, or are you self-aware enough to pause and consider how the old may be impacting your interpretation of the new? Are you able to manage the situation, or do you allow the situation to manage you?

Social intelligence is the degree to which you seek to understand and get along with others. It's the ability to foster conversation, listen nonjudgmentally, read verbal and nonverbal cues, form social bonds, build collaboration and facilitate trust.

The good news is this - research in brain plasticity reveals that intelligence is a process, not a fixed asset. Therefore, leadership is not for the elite or select few. It's not a title or status to reach. Leadership is a behavior. We're all called to exhibit leadership behaviors in our life, at every stage of life. It is our intended state of being to mindfully nurture and steward the gift of life and relationships around us.

Perhaps you've heard the saying, "No [man] is an island." You and I are certainly self-determined, but we're not self-sufficient. We need one another. We were made for relationship. The roles and responsibilities toward each other, our planet, and our own self-care call for the inherent attributes of accountability, supervision, nurturing, guidance, and responsibility to direct healthy, effective, contributory results. You were born into leadership – it's your God-given birthright.

Even the best, most well-established leaders can become more effective! Imagine what you could accomplish with more support, creativity, innovation, and passion from the people around you. THE INFLUENCE ZONE will help you discover new insights, attitudes, and abilities that mobilize colleagues, customers, family and friends through inspiring, motivating, and mutually respectful relationships.

About the Program

It's one thing to read about the traits shared by great, motivational leaders with expansive zones of influence. In THE INFLUENCE ZONE, you'll learn how to assimilate and use their most inspiring behaviors each day toward results-oriented opportunities.

Through daily learning lessons and reflection activities, you'll engage with:

- personal factors influencing your impact on others;
- subconscious triggers that either limit or unleash your leadership potential;
- proven strategies for effective self-management;
- tools to model, mentor, mobilize, and monitor excellence in others;
- diversity factors that spark drive, energy, and creativity from those around you;
- and how culture influences purpose, alignment, innovation and collaboration for next-level living and sustainable results.

Inspirational leadership is a learnable skill. Whether it's in your home, church and/or civic organizations, community, or business, THE INFLUENCE ZONE will help you uncover and integrate leadership intelligence that connects you to the heart of motivating others.

About The Process

If you've read *Growing from Potential to Performance: Creating Transformation by the Renewing of Your Mind*, you're already well acquainted with the most effective ways to utilize and assimilate this information. So jump in and enjoy the experience!

If not, here is important information for getting the most successful, effective, long-lasting impact from this book:

The biggest challenge most people encounter is how they approach this content. Will you simply read for knowledge and inspiration, or will you engage with the reflection activities to gain personal insights into your own behaviors and potential roadblocks to meaningful change in your life? It ultimately comes down to the difference between gaining new information and creating sustainable transformation. That's why I've outlined this book as a 30-day reflective guide for you.

Socrates said, "The unexamined life is not worth living." The ancient psalmist wrote, "Search me, O God, and know my heart; test me and know my anxious thoughts. See if there is any offensive way in me, and lead me in the way of everlasting" (Psalm 139:23-24, The Holy Bible, NIV). Famed columnist Ann Landers penned, "Know yourself. Don't accept your dog's admiration as conclusive evidence that you're wonderful."

Research shows there's no growth without the first step of self-examination. The reflection activities in this book are designed to get you to dig deep and uncover the root of what's driving your current behaviors yielding your current outcomes. The more time you spend getting to the root of your current thinking, the more targeted and effective your change will become. Once you gain the necessary insights, it becomes a simple process of learning how to retrain your brain to take control and manage what's been managing you! In my previous book, *Growing from Potential to Performance: Creating Transformation by the Renewing of Your Mind*, I outline research-based methods to assist in your own personal growth and effectiveness. In *The Influence Zone*, the research and tools are applied to help you better lead and impact others.

Building a daily habit of guided examination to challenge your current thinking and discovering deeper self-awareness by thoughtfully writing out your responses will make all the difference in how fast you see yourself moving closer toward your goals. This 10-minute-a-day exercise each morning will be your first step to successful change and development in the area(s) of your choosing.

A few recommendations for how to get the most out of this scientific and deeply transformational process:

1. Don't make it your goal to get through the book. Make your goal the outcome you want to see, feel, or possess as a result of going through this process. In the first lesson, you'll be asked to identify specific people you want to influence and specific behaviors you want to change or acquire by the end

of 30 days. This will become your focus and intention over the entire journey.

Having a clear target is essential to success. If you aim at nothing, you can count on hitting nothing every time. Therefore, be detailed and descriptive about the change you want to see. While you're quite capable of changing in multiples areas of your life at the same time, I would encourage you to select one specific behavioral goal for the next 30 days. Commit and see it through. Then, as you become more comfortable with the process and familiar with the psychological tools and concepts, you can always go back and address other areas where you'd like to grow.

If you miss a day, that's fine. No pressure. No guilt. Don't put this journey on a "have to" basis. Research shows that living life with a "have to" mindset only creates more stress and anxiety. When that happens, you'll find yourself procrastinating or subconsciously pushing back from completing the process.

Give yourself grace and permission. Commit to a "want to" experience as you look forward to the daily self-discovery and internal mindset shift that takes place over a 30-day investment period.

An effective way to create a "want-to" experience is to envision your specific end result as already achieved or accomplished. Then challenge yourself to list all the benefits or "want-to's" for accomplishing that change – physically, emotionally, relationally, spiritually, financially, and so on. In other words, why do you want this goal? What do you hope to achieve by gaining it? List as many benefits as possible.

Write your end result and benefits on a 3 x 5 card and keep it close by. Review your card each morning upon rising and before you go to sleep at night. The picture of your end result and the emotions or pay value in achieving it will become so compelling that it will motivate you to invest the 10 minutes each day to move you forward toward your future on a consistent basis.

2. The format of this book is based on research and best practices for successful change and growth. So, discipline yourself to only one lesson per day. Faster isn't necessarily better when it comes to self-examination and change. You actually benefit less by taking on multiple days and lessons at one time rather than letting your spirit and subconscious fully work one lesson, complete with reflection questions and activities over the course of your day.

Additionally, the process of this book is not only to create self-discovery – the first step to all meaningful and lasting change – it's to create new habit formation. Research indicates that it takes approximately 21-28 days of consistent, focused, reflective thinking to create a new belief in the neuron cell of the brain. Repetitive thought builds belief. The more you dwell on what it is you want - in the proper way – the greater your likelihood of achieving it. The process of revisiting various aspects of your goal over the next 30 days will help you build that daily discipline and new belief.

3. Because you are fluid and ever-changing, and the circumstances around your life are fluid and ever-changing, the lessons and exercises in this book can be applied to your life over and over again – month after month or year after year.

You will not learn all there is about the human mind or gain complete insight into how and why you behave like you do from one reading of this book at this one particular season of your life. However, if you consistently apply these cognitive principles to your daily circumstances – whatever they may be – you will experience an unfolding of insight that will help to propel you forward. You will cultivate the best practices and mindsets used by most high-performing individuals – that of developing a greater conscious awareness of your subconscious thinking patterns, thereby increasing your likelihood of taking every thought captive to insure it's positive, constructive, and moving you toward your desired outcomes.

To that end, I encourage you to use this book time and again to breathe fresh life into stale outcomes.

4. Lastly, the daily format is constructed by intent. People learn better and retain more effectively when information is presented in story. And old Indian proverb states, "Tell me a fact and I'll learn; tell me a truth and I'll believe; but tell me a story and it will live in my heart forever." Parables, or the power of story, leave a much deeper impression in the heart and mind than facts and figures, alone.

An intriguing or inspirational narrative opens each day and is designed to impact your thinking and help with recall throughout the day. The developmental principle or cognitive concept will follow and help illustrate the point of the story. Then you'll be asked to reflect on how that lesson applies to your current reality and future goal. These questions have been designed to unravel the root cause of ineffective beliefs and behaviors that require your attention for change.

I hope you'll find the flow engaging, interesting, and enlightening. With these recommendations in mind, I wish you all the best as you embark on your **30-Day Journey into THE INFLUENCE ZONE!**

DAY ONE

What's Your Influence Factor?

STORY - A former mentor of mine was invited to England to be the keynote speaker at a special company event. They were a medical supplies organization that had been using our organization's teachings to create a high-performance culture.

They were very excited for his arrival and assembled the senior leadership for a day of activities, including a tour of the facility. As they were passing through the manufacturing floor my mentor was struck by what he saw – rows upon rows of women standing side by side in white overcoats and hairnets, rolling cloth bandages by hand. Intrigued, he stopped the tour and asked to speak to some of the women.

In particular, there was an older lady who had been there several decades. He couldn't imagine the monotony of hand-rolling bandages day in and day out for all those years. When he asked her to describe what she did, she simply looked at him and said, "We relieve human suffering." He was dumbfounded.

He certainly expected to see positive results from his principles taking shape in the company, but the ability of these laborers to possess a larger, nobler purpose beyond their mundane, daily tasks was truly inspirational...and humbling.

He told me, "If you want to evaluate the influence of leadership, don't look for it on a balance sheet; measure the passion and sense of purpose in the people."

CONCEPT - Your ability to interact with and influence people in ways that gain support for your ideas and desired outcomes is the role, the goal, and the challenge of every leader. Your leadership style will either create invested, engaged, self-motivated meaning for others, or it will engender half-hearted, task-oriented efforts that lack life, innovation and vision.

Leadership is a behavior, not a title. It's how you live rather than a role you play. Whether it's in your home, school, community, social circles or profession, how you impact others makes all the difference.

You may have the moxie to execute strategy or the might to manage and control, but inspirational leadership that engages others toward ownership and excellence requires an intelligent heart.

This 30-day journey will give you examples, insights, and tools to expand your ability to win the hearts and minds of those you seek to influence.

INSIGHT - Who, specifically, do you want to influence over the next 30 days? Make a list.

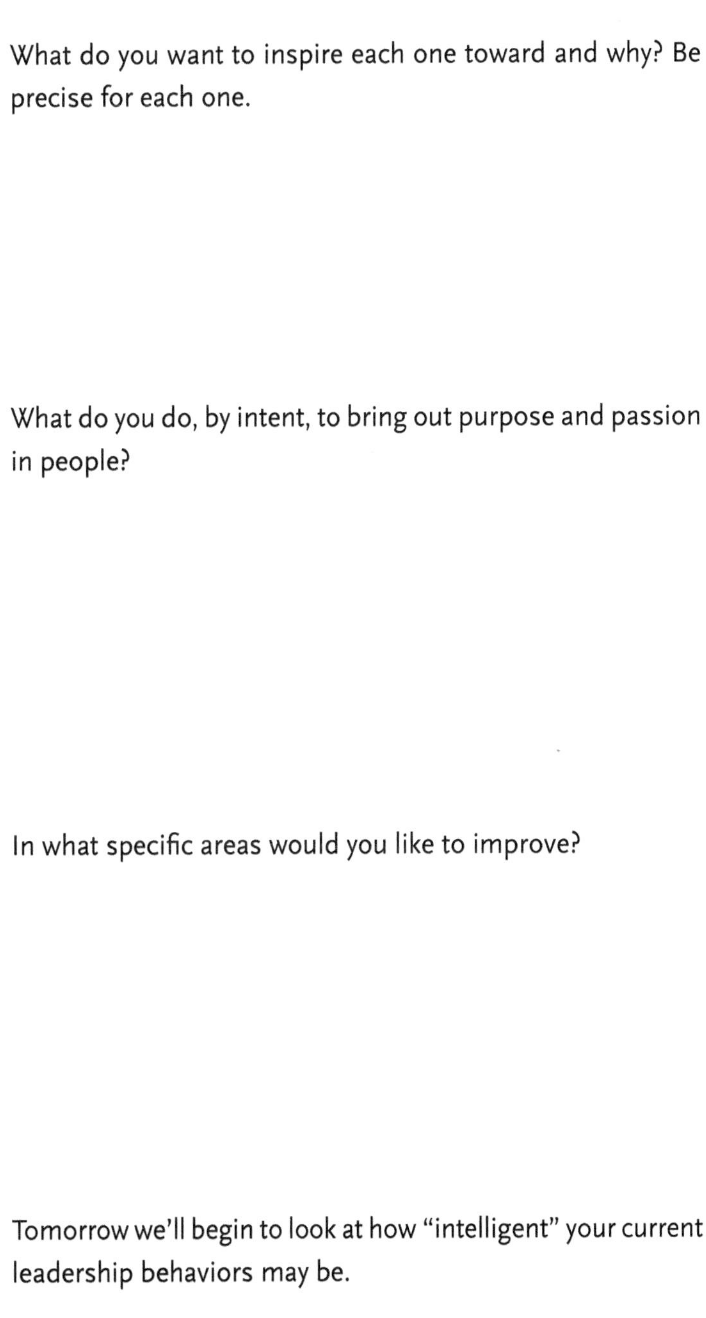

What do you want to inspire each one toward and why? Be precise for each one.

What do you do, by intent, to bring out purpose and passion in people?

In what specific areas would you like to improve?

Tomorrow we'll begin to look at how "intelligent" your current leadership behaviors may be.

DAY TWO

The Heart of Leadership

STORY - I was working with a firm who had a leader that others avoided. He was legal counsel for the business and was a smart but domineering, forceful guy.

The associates loved when he was defending their clients. His argumentative, aggressive manner often won the case. But the strengths of his courtroom counterpunches were often weaknesses with his peer relationships. In the office, he was known for being brash, dismissive, opinionated, and condescending. Whether or not he was aware, he shut other people down.

Interestingly, he viewed his demeanor as normal, positive, and appropriate. It was consistent with the cultural norms of his upbringing. His mantra? "What you see is what you get. You always know where I stand."

The problem was he only had half of the relationship equation... HIM! His outspoken candidness left no room for the feelings and contributions of others. Company creativity, innovation, and progress suffered by his callous need to always be heard and always be right. Eventually, his colleagues shut down and stopped trying.

CONCEPT - In 1995, Daniel Goleman's best-selling book popularized the concept of Emotional Intelligence – the ability to effectively perceive, interpret, and respond to your emotions in order to guide constructive thinking and behavior. Along with intellectual know-how, leaders who are self-aware with strong emotional and social intelligence know how to optimize interaction with others to positively influence their response.

Your effectiveness in guiding the actions and intentions of others will only be as good as your awareness, understanding, and constructive self-management over your own attitudes and emotions. If you want to expand your influence zone, you need more than just head-smarts; you need a smart heart.

John Eldredge writes that the heart is the center of life that requires the mind – not the other way around. Desire – rooted in the heart or spirit – is what gets people to move. We may intellectually know the truth or the reasonable thing to do, but action, creativity, and excellence arrive when we connect to and motivate from the heart, the fount of our desires.

INSIGHT - On a scale from 1 (-) to 10 (+), how would you rate your overall emotional intelligence? Use your interactions today to become consciously aware of how much emotional intelligence you apply to each relationship. Score yourself and jot it down. It's hard to manage and hold yourself accountable to what you don't measure.

List some ways you can improve your daily interactions with each person for the next time.

Influential leadership is rooted in the idea that achievement isn't based on what you know but on getting yourself and others to do what you know on a regular, consistent basis. That requires an intelligent heart that keeps motivation alive.

This program is designed to help you gain greater awareness, understanding, and management of your own emotional motivations so you can lead others with greater intelligence, effectiveness, persuasion, purpose and passion.

Tomorrow we'll begin the journey of awareness.

DAY THREE

Carrying the Weight of Your Past

STORY - A wise teacher gave his students a leadership lesson. He handed each a burlap sack and had them fill it with one stone for each offense they could recall over their lifetime. Soon, the conscious remembering of stored transgressions caused their sacks to become full and quite heavy.

When the students reconvened, the teacher said, "And now your lesson begins." He instructed them to carry their sacks everywhere they went for the next 30 days.

At first the students tried to bear up under this leadership challenge. But soon their strength gave way to discomfort, weariness, and even physical pain. The reality of waking each day to their burdensome sack made some depressed and complacent.

Others became angry, cynical, and critical of those without sacks who didn't appear to be working as hard. Most were easily frustrated and irritable with people and things around them. They were growing impatient, resentful, and ready to rid themselves of the unwanted weight.

At the end of thirty days, the teacher asked what lessons they had learned.

First – The sacks represent the emotional baggage we carry with us every day.

Second – The burden of these past offenses weighs on our present perspectives and influences our daily attitudes, abilities, and actions.

Third – Unless we intentionally release the weight of negative emotions, we continue to accumulate them until we're no longer efficient and effective at handling life.

"Well done," the teacher said. "For now you see the strength of life and leadership is not in the weight-bearing capacity of what you can hold, but in discerning what to let go.

CONCEPT - Whether you're accused of showing too much emotion or condemned for not showing enough, we all carry emotional baggage that impacts the release of our potential and the results of our performance.

Emotional memory and emotional habits don't go away. They're imprinted and stored in the neuron cells of the brain. They become your automatic "default drive" when circumstances appear contradictory, challenging, or stressful. Learning how to manage them effectively is the key.

INSIGHT - On a scale from 1 (low) to 10 (high), how heavy is your emotional baggage?

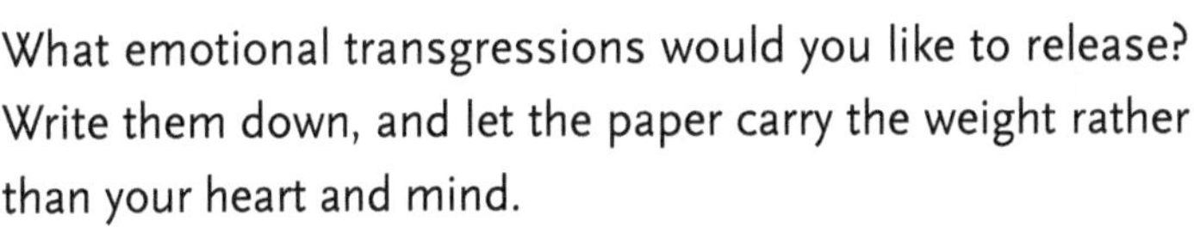

What emotional transgressions would you like to release? Write them down, and let the paper carry the weight rather than your heart and mind.

Think about qualities you want to be known for? If someone was writing your leadership epitaph, what would you want it to say?

How you carry the weight of your past will determine the quality of success, satisfaction, and significance in your future. Tomorrow I'll share the three pillars necessary to construct a solid foundation for life and leadership.

DAY FOUR

Learning to Live in Alignment

STORY - Jason Brown, #60, was one of the best centers in the National Football League. The former Baltimore Ravens and St. Louis Rams lineman possessed a disciplined mindset and strong body. But in 2011, Brown shocked the NFL by walking away from a five-year, $37 million contract in order to farm!

Though he'd never farmed a day in his life, he bought 1000 acres and learned by watching YouTube videos. Critics said it would be the worst mistake of his life. Brown says, "I've never felt more successful – not in man's standards, but in God's eyes."

He named his farm "First Fruits" because he donates the first harvest to nearby food pantries. When asked why he would leave fame and fortune in the height of his career, he said, "When I think about a life of greatness, I think about a life of service...and love is the most wonderful currency you can give anyone."

CONCEPT - We are more than physical, intellectual beings – your body is home to your mind and spirit. The spirit births purpose, motivation, and positive intention. The mind assesses and determines your potential. The body manifests or displays your intentions and thinking in real performance.

It takes all three to optimize effectiveness. It involves all three to live healthy and whole. When you exclude or ignore one area, you compromise the full capacity of your God-given, intended state of being.

Embracing a holistic purpose is the foundation for leadership intelligence. Your interior life must be just as important and evident as your exterior performance. Otherwise, it's an uphill battle to inspire others toward something that's not authentic in your own heart.

INSIGHT - Think about the kind of life you want to live – spiritually, mentally, and physically. Make a column for each and write down the emotional & behavioral characteristics you'd like to live by under each category.

Do you notice any patterns or common phrases? Pay attention and write them down. It might be your heart's way of communicating missing, wanted, or depleted needs.

You're not one-dimensional. You are triune in nature – body, mind, and spirit. Likewise, your thoughts and attitudes aren't one-dimensional. They have spiritual, psychological, and physiological consequences impacting your purpose, potential, and performance – not only for you, but also for those you influence.

When you experience physical disease or emotional dis-ease, they're external symptoms indicating you're out of internal alignment with your intended nature. Tomorrow I'll share new scientific intelligence on the power of alignment to influence the environments around you.

DAY FIVE

Mapping Your Flow of Influence

STORY - Adam Grant is an organizational psychologist and known for having been the youngest, most highly rated professor at Wharton School of Business.

In his New York Times bestselling book, *Give and Take*, Grant provides compelling content disproving the notion that competitive, self-protecting, self-promoting, me-first, "Takers" dominate in business success.

In fact, it's those with characteristics of "Givers" who are often top performers, averaging 50% more annual revenue than "Takers" or "Matchers" – those who give in equal measure to what they get.

CONCEPT - While we often expect to find Givers in the helping professions, Givers in business support success in others, share information, and don't hijack credit for themselves. Though they can be perceived as too caring, trusting, and naïve, research shows their advantage grows over time.

They create connections in which networking, collaboration, and influencing are strengths that others seek out in them. In their concern for the well-being of others, they expand their own knowledge-base and skill sets.

In one study, social networking researchers mapped the flow of energy leaders produced through their interactions. Employees rated their connections with leaders on a scale from "strongly energizing" to "strongly de-energizing." Their findings? The energy network map of Givers resembled the look of the galaxy.

By contrast, the network map of Takers resembled a "black hole [that] sucked energy from those around them. Meanwhile, Givers were suns [who] injected light around the organization."

The other-focused, spirit-driven leadership of Givers encouraged and respected the contributions of others, building and bringing out the best in the people around them.

INSIGHT - Who would you identify as some of the greatest giving, other-centered, spirit-driven leaders that have impacted you throughout your life?

What qualities did they possess that made them so influential?

Which ones would you like to incorporate more into your own leadership behaviors?

Be proactive! List a few "Giver" activities you can do today with specific people or in your daily functions. Actively look for opportunities to model those behaviors. If you don't use them, you'll eventually lose them.

Employing the attributes of Givers in life and leadership requires an unconditional esteem for others; a vulnerability to contribute without measure; and an effective handle on your own intentions and emotions.

The quality with which you manage your emotions will determine the quantity of happiness, peace, and health in your own life, as well as the zone of influence around you. Tomorrow I'll share a subconscious snare that often gets in the way.

DAY SIX

The Hidden Power of Emotions

STORY - In one of my sessions, I asked how many people like music. All hands rose. Then I asked how many people like to sing? One lady emphatically retracted her hand, so I knew she was the perfect target.

I asked her to come up and join me in a little song. She physically recoiled and winced, stating that she could not sing. When I asked what happened to her vocal chords, she clarified that she wasn't good at singing. I asked her how she knew.....in other words, where did that belief first originate?

After some thought, she recounted an incident in music class in the second grade. As all the children were happily singing, the teacher abruptly stopped the song to locate the offensive, off-pitch student. The music teacher singled her out in front of all her classmates to tell her she was out of key. She was then instructed to mouth the words, but not give voice to the song.

From that day forward, she never sang. She affirmed the belief that she couldn't sing. Even though she was now an adult, even though she loved to worship in church, she only mouthed the words. Any opportunity to use her voice still triggered emotions of inadequacy, judgment, and humiliation.

CONCEPT - Every experience you've ever encountered has been recorded in your brain. Additionally, how you felt about it is stored in the amygdala – the emotion center of the brain. In fact, emotion is an essential ingredient for building memory.

The beliefs you call "truth" or "reality" for you, are formed by your own thoughts plus the intensity of emotion associated with them, along with the amount of replay you entertain in your mind.

That means, you don't need multiple experiences of the same negative event to build a strong belief. With just one event, you have 86,400 seconds in each day to nurse, rehearse, and replay one emotional experience into a powerful reality for you, even if it's far below the raw potential you possess.

INSIGHT - Think of a significant emotional experience from your past. Journal the emotional memories that imprinted in your brain as a result.

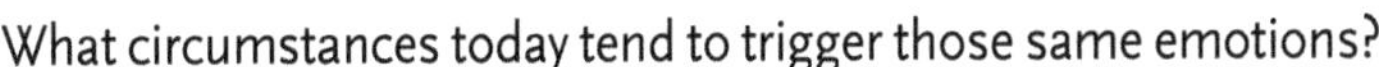
What circumstances today tend to trigger those same emotions?

Become more mindful of when those triggers are causing you to aggressively react or passively avoid certain situations. The more you're aware of emotional memory hijacks, the better you'll be at preventing them in the future.

Emotional memory is so powerful and familiar to you that you can justify your actions even if they negatively impact your ultimate outcomes.

Conscious awareness of these subconscious triggers is the first step to turning reactive attitudes into proactive solutions.

Tomorrow we'll look at the first of three factors that determine the subconscious emotional response patterns impacting your life and leadership.

DAY SEVEN

IT'S A FAMILY AFFAIR

STORY - There are three factors that go into forming your emotional style. If you've ever been in an "opposites attract" relationship, this first one may sound familiar to you.

My husband and his family have middle-America, German, farming roots. They're hard-working. Nothing gets them too riled up. They're always such a polite, positive, and pleasant group. I've often said, if a dead elephant were lying in the middle of the room, they'd all sit around chatting about the weather and the niceties of the world.

My family, on the other hand, doesn't do so well monitoring the connection between what's in our heads and what comes out of our mouths.

We're passionate – on both ends of love/anger spectrum. If we had a dead elephant in the middle of the room, we'd be talking over one another and pointing fingers at how it got there; whose fault it is; and who's now responsible for getting it out. Then we'd get up and have dinner or play cards like nothing ever happened.

CONCEPT - Your upbringing has everything to do with how you manage your emotions – even if you feel you act in stark contrast to your family.

Unless you've worked consciously and intentionally to change your style, you often continue to mirror and reinforce what you've assimilated as "normal" for you.

More than that, you will subconsciously justify your "normal" as better, healthier, more effective and advantageous than other styles of emotional behavior. It also becomes your default response in leadership, parenting, social relationships, decision-making and more.

Your past conditioning formed the emotional foundations for who you are today. It's those foundations that are responsible for driving your behavior - both constructively and defensively.

INSIGHT - Think about your upbringing and the dominant emotional styles you experienced from parents, siblings, extended family or cultural heritage. Write them all down – both constructive and defensive styles.

Where do these emotional patterns show up today in your dealings with family, team members, and social situations?

List where they have a positive impact and where they negatively impact interactions with those you seek to influence.

Part of your emotion management is learned. It came from watching those in authority over you, as well as your responses to their behaviors.

The patterns you adopted allowed you to function, fit in, or simply survive your circumstances. You knew them to be "normal" even if they were hurtful and harmful to you. Left unchecked, they can become toxic to your overall health, well-being and relationships.

Tomorrow we'll look at the second factor impacting the quality and quantity of your emotional responses.

DAY EIGHT

It's In Your Nature

STORY - Learned behavior from your past conditioning is a huge factor in your emotion management, but a second factor equally applies – your genetic wiring or first nature.

For example, my husband's an engineer. He prides himself on the superiority and efficiency of an analytical mind that's all about logic. He has little time or space for the drama of emotion. It's all about risk-assessment and risk-management.

He's really not THAT dry. He's actually quite funny and lots of fun. But he certainly lives comfortably in the land of left-brain thinking; while I, on the other hand, live dominantly as a right-brain processor. I think and feel deeply about people and situations. I am fiercely loyal and endlessly inquisitive about why we're here, why we behave as we do, and how our worldviews have impacted culture throughout history.

CONCEPT - Research suggests that different sides or hemispheres of the brain control different manners of thinking. And while some people are universal in using each side equally, most of us have a dominant side we use for processing thought and information.

The left brain is more objective, logical, sequential, and analytical. It breaks down the parts to understand the whole. Dominant left-brain thinkers are more exacting and do well in engineering, law, logistics, mathematics, and the sciences.

Right-brain thinkers are more subjective, synthesizing and intuitive. They're able to mix and blend easily. They use feeling, creativity, and aesthetics to produce and relate. They begin with the whole in mind to put context to the parts.

While right-brain thinkers are often more comfortable, expressive, and obvious with their feelings, neither nature is better or more failsafe from defensive and destructive emotions.

INSIGHT - Are you more left-brain or right-brain in your thinking? List the ways your wiring has been a benefit for you and begin to think of how you can intentionally expand those strengths.

Now list ways or circumstances in which you could be limited by your dominant nature. Turn those limitations around by describing in detail a preferred response that might garner more beneficial outcomes.

Understanding your thought processing preferences is no excuse for demanding behavior or over-dramatic antics. It's simply a barometer for your emotional tendencies when left unchecked. As with most things in life, balance is key; and choice of response belongs to you.

Tomorrow we'll discuss the third factor that forms your emotional foundations for life and leadership.

DAY NINE

Finding Your Heart's Desires

STORY - I do an exercise with groups where I give participants an 8-1/2 x 11 sheet of blank paper. I have them fold it in half, then fold again, and again two more times. When they open it, they have four rows of four folded squares each, for a total of sixteen blank squares on the front and sixteen on the back.

Next, I give them 90 seconds to fill in each square with something they want. It could be emotional, physical, spiritual; tangible or intangible; short term or long term. Anything.... no parameters.

I also tell them that when they complete the first sheet, raise their hand for another. In over two decades, I've yet to provide a second sheet of paper, nor has anyone ever filled both sides.

Most people complete the first row, maybe two, but then slow down and struggle. When given the opportunity to dream, they find they've lost or given up on most of their inner-most desires.

CONCEPT - The third factor influencing your emotion management, and the one over which you have the most control, is your life experiences and how you've allow them to impact your heart's desires.

Life happens; disappointment hurts; and the heart remembers. Dr. Marty Seligman, founder of Positive Psychology said, "It's not our failures that determine our future success, but how we explain them to ourselves."

The same is true of pain, grief, and disappointment. It takes conscious effort to reframe life's challenges so they don't take us down the paths of disengagement, disdain, depression or despair where we no longer dare to dream.

INSIGHT - Take the "Dare to Dream" challenge for yourself. Find an 8-1/2 x 11 sheet of paper. Fold it in half and then again three more times. Time yourself for 90 seconds and fill in the sixteen squares on each side of the paper with things you desire. When done, reflect on the exercise. Was it easy? Uncomfortable? Inspiring? Challenging? Frustrating? Sad?

Once you've identified your emotional response, ask yourself, "Why did this experience make me feel that way?" Jot down your insights.

It's basic instinct to shield oneself from perceived pain and danger. But beware you don't permit past pains to subconsciously stifle future possibilities.

Every day you make assumptions and draw conclusions about yourself, others, and the world around you. In part, those conclusions are rooted in stored memory. The more aware you are of their impact, the better your decisions will be.

Tomorrow I'll highlight the decision-making process so you can lead with greater accuracy and influence.

DAY TEN

RELIVING THE PAST

STORY -In fourth grade I moved to a new state where my accent was quite distinct from the other kids. When I read aloud in class, they laughed at my pronunciation of particular words. Additionally my teacher tried to keep me from talking with my hands – a trait common in my expressive Italian family. So she had me sit on my hands when I spoke.

Eventually I became so nervous and self-conscious about public speaking that I'd lose my train of thought right in mid-sentence, which evoked even more embarrassment. Though I was recognized and rewarded for my writing, I determined I was horrible at verbal communication, and I hated the sound of my voice.

I declined every opportunity to "be out front," telling myself I was a behind-the-scenes person. I was in my 40's before I retrained my thinking to believe I had something of value to say that people longed to hear.

CONCEPT - Each time you encounter new information or opportunities, the first thing your mind looks for is context. "What does this mean? Does this new information look familiar to me? Have I experienced anything like this before?" It triggers memory, looking for an association between the new information and any previously stored experiences.

It moves next to your amygdala, the emotion database in your brain, to see how you felt about those past experiences. It then begins evaluating or deliberating over probable outcomes: Will this new opportunity be good or bad, helpful or harmful, effective or destructive?

The stronger the association and emotional memory from the past, the greater the likelihood you'll base your new decisions, not on the potential of what could be, but on the history of what has happen before.

INSIGHT - Recall your last few major decisions and the thought analysis you used. How much of your past experiences influenced those decisions?

Now that you understand the decision-making process, how might your decisions have changed?

Write out steps for how you will make more effective decisions in the future?

If you judge the probability of your future solely on the emotional memory of your past, you'll stunt your potential and miss amazing opportunities for abundant life. To travel forward into new paths, you must consciously untether from the past.

Knowing that your mind naturally defaults to stored emotional memory now gives you the power to choose. You don't have to react based on history; you can manage your future with greater clarity, accountability, and purpose.

DAY ELEVEN

Where You Live is How You'll Lead

STORY - I was coaching a man who was in a transitional point in his life and leadership. Though successful, he felt trapped and dissatisfied. I eventually learned his career choice was motivated more from a strained relationship with his father than a desire to work in that field. He was competitive, closed up, and had pushed other people away while trying to prove something to someone who wasn't even paying attention – his father. Now decades later he felt stuck, with no passion for the work he was doing.

Conversely, I worked with a woman who came from a terribly dysfunctional family. She married into the same kind of abuses she encountered as a child. Rather than build barriers, she had too few boundaries. She was a people-pleaser who always took the path of least resistance and then felt taken advantage of by family, friends, and colleagues.

Both individuals were driven by the need for approval, but found different ways to control their lives in order to protect their hearts.

CONCEPT - Whether we refuse to feel or feel too much, protective emotions yield defensive behaviors that always trap our true potential. We wind up spending much of our energy and our very life running from fear rather than running toward vision.

Vision is faith. It's a clear and confident assurance in the things you hope for but don't yet see.

When you live authentically from faith, you lead effectively toward vision. You consistently set a direction that's future-focused *without* fear.

You inspire and influence others by painting a vivid, meaningful picture of the end result that highlights the benefits and positive expectation that others long to see.

INSIGHT - Where are you currently dissatisfied and why?

Take your response and ask "why" again. Then take that response and continue the process of asking "why." Then ask yourself when you first remember having that belief. Eventually, this line of questioning will lead you to unravel and discover the root fear managing that particular area of your life.

Release it and replace it with a positive vision statement. Write it down and read it twice a day for the next 30 days. You'll re-engineer your expectations toward healthy, positive, constructive results.

All emotional responses can be boiled down to two major types: fear-based or faith-based reactions.

Purposeful, faith-based discontent of the status quo leads toward a vision that inspires engagement, innovation, progress and endurance in others.

Fear-based discontent focuses on what we don't have and don't want. It creates a stress-filled environment that limits potential.

Tomorrow I'll explain how.

DAY TWELVE

The Stress of Fear-Based Emotions

STORY - We all know stress is bad, but did you know that nearly 87% of major diseases have their roots in stress?

That's because your body functions like a 911 emergency system that responds to the threat of survival. The dispatch center, your endocrine system, alerts first responders - those hormones like adrenaline and cortisol that enable you to react or retreat quickly. Blood pressure, heart rate, glucose levels, lactic acid, and more, rush into emergency service. Inflammation is heightened, policing your body for injury so it can come to your healing aid.

These responses are effective for acute stress where there's a rapid onset of threat but a normalizing after danger is dismissed. They aren't meant to sustain you under the constant pressure of emotional stress or distress.

Entertaining chronic negative emotions is like putting your 911 responders on active duty, high alert, 24/7. The constant overdrive and overtime are taxing on the body. Eventually systems break down manifesting in various types of emotional dis-ease or physical disease.

Chronic emotional stress isn't just ineffective emotion management; it's a matter of life or death.

CONCEPT - Your thought life is tied to your biology. The hypothalamus is the pumping station in your brain that secretes chemicals matching your emotion state.

Unmanaged, fear-based emotions like worry, anxiety, anger, bitterness, frustration, resentment, guilt, shame, humiliation, and hate build up a toxic environment that compromises and changes your internal feedback loops and immune functions right down to the cellular level.

INSIGHT- On a scale from 1-10, (with 1- low and 10-high) how would you rate your recent stress levels?

Today, become more aware of toxic emotions that are exhausting your body's 911 functions. List a few things you can do to intentionally let them go. The more consciously proactive you are, the less subconsciously enslaved you will be.

Stress triggers in life are inevitable; disease doesn't have to be. Your body goes into 911 mode to help you fight, flight or freeze during momentary danger. But sustained stress eventually wears you down and affects your leadership influence.

Holistic emotion management includes proper self-care management. Tomorrow we'll look at helpful and hurtful habits impacting your body's physiological ability to manage stress. The activities you choose will help to feed it or free it.

DAY THIRTEEN

How You Feed Your Feelings

STORY - In 1996 I had my own Forrest Gump moment. In the movie, actor Tom Hanks plays Forrest Gump who encounters deep emotional trauma. To deal with the overwhelming pain, he takes off running. And so did I.

It was a horrible year where my friend, my father, and my grandmother all died unexpectedly within one month of each other. A love relationship ended, and then my mother had a near-fatal car collision which took months of healing and rehabilitation. I was alone and living across the country, away from family support. I couldn't bear the emotional loneliness and misery any longer. So one day I started to run. Even though I wasn't a "runner," I just kept running. Every day I would run and run until my physical exhaustion exceeded my emotional exhaustion.

Eventually I became emotionally and physically stronger. Thankfully, running became a healthy, cathartic choice for me.

CONCEPT - Most unhealthy habits begin as mental distractions, keeping you from focusing on what you're actually feeling. Activities like smoking, drinking, drugs, sex, work, TV, shopping, gambling, and eating, can be used as self-defeating devises to soothe unresolved emotions.

Though you may not suffer from obvious addictions, taking proactive steps to form healthy habits enhances your ability to manage your moods and influence others.

A very effective habit is living consciously – becoming mindful of emotional triggers and your response to them.

- Journaling is a great way to examine subconscious emotional patterns and release pent-up tensions.
- Good nutrition and a balanced diet will keep your glucose levels stable, maximizing energy and minimizing mood swings.
- Daily exercise, like walking, releases serotonin and other feel-good endorphins that enhance memory and mindset.
- Proper sleep promotes healthy cell function that enhances your immune system.
- Prayer, meditation, and deep breathing help you release disappointments of the past and fears of the future so you can live fully present in the moment.
- An accountability partner always helps to keep you honest and on track.

INSIGHT - Create two lists of healthy and unhealthy ways you typically deal with stressful negative emotions.

Review the unhealthy column. What healthy responses will you choose now to replace the unhealthy ones? Commit and write them down.

You can feed negative emotions with unhealthy choices or you can be proactive by creating a self-care system that gives your body the leading edge in managing stress.

The ability to monitor your own spiritual, emotional, and physical cues will ignite your perception and enhance your aptitude for mentoring others.

In the next several messages we move from understanding your own behavioral leadership styles to the second step for expanding your influence zone – discerning the mindset and understanding the motivations of those you lead, otherwise known as social intelligence.

DAY FOURTEEN

Motivation.... Whose Business Is It Anyway?

STORY - I was reading a running dialogue on a popular and prestigious online business publication. The discussion was titled, "How to Motivate Yourself When Your Boss Doesn't." I figured I'd see great tips and tools offered by seasoned professionals.

Instead, I was stunned by the responses. Senior-level contributors commented that it's not the boss' job to keep you engaged. You need to motivate yourself or get a coach who can help you.

One commenter added that if you're not happy, go somewhere else. There are plenty of good people out there who would want your job!

CONCEPT - To be sure, leaders shouldn't have to perform inspirational acrobatics to keep people pumped up about their work. If leaders effectively communicate vision, expectations, and outcomes, and equip people with the necessary skills, resources, and compensation, then the accountability to perform rests on the employee.

But consider the consequences of the annual Gallup Global Workplace Study where 87% of employees, worldwide, feel disengaged from their work, and 70% of U.S. employees report the same. Sadly, these findings are nothing new. For the past few decades these U.S. statistics have remained relatively steady.

Now factor in the economics from this lack of engagement. Studies show that disengaged employees cost companies between 35-50% of payroll. That means 70% are disengaged employees being paid 100% of their salary but withholding 35-50% of what they're capable of contributing!

Individual accountability and responsibility is essential in work and in all of life. But ignoring social intelligence and motivational leadership yields a deficit that organizations simply can't afford to make.

INSIGHT - Connect with one person today who would benefit most from your personal time and attention. Acknowledge a strength or characteristic you value in them that's contributory to the success of the whole. Be authentic in your assessment and jot down what you notice about their response.

Consider selecting one new person each day with whom you'll build intentional rapport and influence. Write down one name for each day of the week to stay on track and accountable.

Whether you're a parent, coach, or boss, tension exists between the need for external motivation and one's own internal drive to perform.

Additionally, your personality type influences how natural and normal it is for you to be nurturing, mentoring, and intentionally inspirational.

So tomorrow we'll look at how dominant personality styles shape your interaction with others and how you can influence more effectively by becoming more aware of who it is you're talking to.

DAY FIFTEEN

Do You Know Who You're Talking To?

STORY - Chris was the ultimate salesman. His parents had been affirming that fact from the time he was five years old.

His high energy, dominant nature and fast talking, negotiating skills left little doubt he'd be a success. His strategy was to fill the sales funnel, make his pitch, and churn through the numbers.

John was more reserved. He spent time listening, educating, and making connections. In some cases, he sent customers away to seek out other options.

This horrified Chris, and he quickly outpaced John in closings for the first few years. But eventually his sales leveled off, while John held long-term customers and built referrals.

Both Chris and John were successful influencers, but John's strategy ended up reaping higher long-term rewards. Rather than play the sales game of overriding customer objections, John knew to adjust his presentations based on reading his customer's needs and demeanor.

CONCEPT - Successful influencers aren't as focused on pushing their own message as they are with understanding who it is they're talking to and communicating in a way to build trust.

Profiling tools, like DISC, Myers Briggs, B.A.N.K., and The Big Five, help assess and characterize different behavioral types.

In general, people fall into one of four dominate categories: action-oriented, analytical, empathetic-nurturers, or systematic planners. These styles impact decision-making choices.

Chris' "act now" approach didn't always appeal to analytical buyers who value facts and figures. It didn't feel authentic to the empathic nurturers. It was too hyped up without enough structure for planners. Chris' best customers? Other action-oriented buyers who spoke his language.

INSIGHT - Which of the four behavioral styles do you favor or feel is most natural for you?

As you think about the individuals you want to influence, how aware are you of their dominant styles and preferences? Make a list of names and use your judgment to discern their style. If you're unsure, ask them!

When you interact with people today, pause to consider whether your approach aligns with their subconscious preferences or if it tends to create pushback in others.

Your verbal and non-verbal cues communicate values and intentions that others subconsciously filter and evaluate against their own value systems. When those values match, people respond. When they don't, people back away.

Learning to identify and speak to different processing styles will make you much more effective in sharing your ideas and motivating others to take action.

In addition to personality differences, generational values also impact your influence zone. Tomorrow, we'll see how.

DAY SIXTEEN

Influencing Across the Divide

STORY - My friend is a business owner who interviews applicants even when he doesn't have an opening. He's a student of culture and likes to stay current on trends taking place in the employment pool.

He's noticed a shift in values and expectations that many older employers are grappling with – the generational diversity of the new, younger workforce.

Many organizational leaders today are Baby Boomers, born 1946-1964. Known as the ME generation, they live to work, seek to acquire, and focus on achievement.

They differ from the Gen Xers, born 1965-82. Labelled the "lost generation," these latchkey kids grew up with divorce and daycare. They're highly educated, but skeptical. They work to live and focus on relationships.

Newer to the workforce are the Millennials, born 1983-2002. They're a paradox of being sheltered yet pressured; isolated yet globally connected; worldly yet protected. They're multitaskers who are quickly bored, distracted, and impatient.

Millennials don't simply accept prevailing authorities and value systems. They have a "shop around" attitude where life is a virtual catalogue of choices at their fingertips. Generation Z, coming behind them, shares these characteristics even more.

CONCEPT - Motivating and leading the younger workforce requires a new approach, says Dr. Tim Elmore, author of *"Generation iY: Our Last Chance to Save Their Future."*

These are young people who were conditioned to receive rewards for simply showing up. Moms socialized their play dates. They have their own TV networks, apps, and social media catering directly to them.

Employers are finding that entry-level positions, compensation based on contribution, and working their way to the top aren't part of the Millennial mindset. They expect to already be there!

INSIGHT - What cultural or generational attitudes do you find present in your home or work?

How do those attitudes differ from yours? In what ways do they align? Focus on the strengths and similarities and use them to win trust and guide positive outcomes.

We live in an increasingly shrinking world where personality, cultural, and generational differences confront us every day.

Influential leadership learns, recognizes, and effectively responds to these differences while having the capability to guide diverse people toward their highest contribution for the common good and common goal.

Your success will depend largely on identifying what drives individuals at their core – the pursuit of happiness. Tomorrow we'll look at the four levels of happiness that unite us despite our diversity.

DAY SEVENTEEN

Four Levels of Happiness

STORY - Aristotle defined man's purpose or reason for being as the pursuit of happiness to be achieved within the exercise of virtue. He classified happiness into four levels that motivate our behavior:

Level One happiness is the intense but short-lived goal of sensory gratification - pursuing pleasure from things like a good meal, sex, drugs and alcohol, or the rush of adventure. We naturally enjoy physical pleasure, but when Level One indulgences become the only driver of satisfaction, individuals get stuck in shallow lives, living for the short-lived thrill of the moment.

Level Two is ego gratification – being better, smarter, richer, or more admired than others. Level Two fuels progress but when it's the dominant motivator, people become competitive, dividing the world into winners or losers.

Level Three is contributory gratification. Self-sacrifice, compassion, forgiveness and serving satisfy this level. Individuals are motivated by a higher, nobler purpose outside their own interests.

Level Four is seeking the ultimate and infinite source of love, life, truth, and peace.

CONCEPT - When a society, organization, or family is built on Level One or Level Two attitudes, people become a means to an end. Organizations get lulled into the illusion that the cunning and competitive have the strongest qualities to lead. Leadership becomes "might is right." Individuals become withholding and protective of their own interests.

Leadership intelligence that ignites results looks for Level Three influencers who naturally model and mentor behaviors that seek the best ends for the most good.

They communicate compelling vision that stirs others to action. They exude authenticity because they genuinely seek a shared and common happiness achieved through the exercise of virtue or high moral standards.

INSIGHT - As you move through your day, become mindful of your motivations. Tonight, schedule a quick "day-end debrief" with yourself to reflect on what levels of happiness you pursued in your activities.

Envision what you'll do tomorrow to live, work, and interact from a place of Level Three leadership. Jot down your ideas so you don't forget them in the busyness of tomorrow.

Level Three leaders help others discover deeper meaning, purpose, and vision in their daily routines - like the organization with the ladies rolling bandages in our very first message.

Level Three organizations outperform others because they intentionally create a culture of care and commonality that ignites commitment.

Tomorrow, we'll dig deeper into the foundations of culture to show you what specific leadership behaviors influence the best results in others.

DAY EIGHTEEN

Are You Satisfied or Secure?

STORY - Drs. Cooke and Lafferty created one of the most widely used and respected tools for measuring organizational behaviors. The Circumplex uncovers and quantifies leadership values that shape cultural norms which influence each member's personal styles and, ultimately, collective productivity and effectiveness.

The tool categorizes three distinct behavior sets: one set of constructive behaviors arising from the need for higher-order satisfaction, and two groups of defensive styles – passive or aggressive – both arising from needs for security.

Leaders who behave constructively from satisfaction needs create cultures where others eagerly take on risks, set goals, cooperate, develop others, and emphasize quality and integrity. They reinforce high rewards and low punishment. Activities are proactive, interactive and flexible. They value collaborative problem-solving and doing good for others.

But if a leader is driven from security needs, he'll either act passively to please people or aggressively to control them – limiting high performance.

CONCEPT - Most leaders aren't aware of subconscious needs driving their behaviors. But most organizations prove to have predominantly defensive cultures.

Aggressive leadership displays perfectionistic, oppositional, competitive, and power-oriented traits. The more forcefully they protect their own status and security, the more they create passive responses in their people who become conforming, avoidant, dependent, and approval-seeking.

While aggressive leaders are self-promoting, passive leaders are self-protecting. They try so hard to be liked that they're often too accommodating, risk avoidant, and ambiguous in their direction with others.

As leaders shift from the need for security to the desire for satisfaction, performance soars because they afford others the same opportunity to express and expand their own satisfaction needs while working toward the success of the organization.

INSIGHT - Security is a fear-based attitude manifesting in the need to control. The less you *"have to"* manage, the better you can *"choose to"* lead.

Pay attention today and capture below what incidences caused you to tighten your grip. Try to isolate what triggered your reactions?

What root-cause beliefs do you hold that are supporting or legitimizing those fear-based responses?

Culture is contagious. It can affect and infect your beliefs, habits, attitudes, and expectations so you can fit in. So powerful is culture that Peter Drucker, the father of modern management, said, "Culture eats strategy for breakfast."

Many leaders are hired into their positions and inherit cultures that have long been established. The legacy thinking embedded in the organization can make for a daunting task of influencing others to release deep security fears for higher-order satisfactions.

Tomorrow I'll show a key to that success.... how you embrace authority.

DAY NINETEEN

Using Your Authority to Serve

STORY -I was the keynote speaker at the gala opening of a major cancer center. They had read my books on the power of faith and healing and wanted me to address 160 of their oncology doctors, staff, and top donors.

They invited me to arrive early in the day to tour the facility. Every part of the design, layout, and materials was purposefully constructed to exude warmth, tranquility, and healing. But as impressed as I was with the physical environment, I was even more intrigued with the people.

Two Senior Vice Presidents cleared their schedules to tour me around. I noticed how genuinely warm and affirming they were with one another. When we encountered custodians, technicians, or staff along the way, they knew each person's name, and stopped to introduce me to them by honoring the contributions each were making to this healing facility.

I was amazed. They displayed a leadership quality I often teach, but don't readily see, in organizations. It became clear when I met the CEO. He was a man who exercised his authority through a spirit of humility and honoring others.

CONCEPT - Humility isn't soft and spineless leadership. It's a proper regard for and stewardship of one's rank without *requiring* respect from one's position. It takes confidence and strength of character to elevate the contributions of others without fearing it will diminish yours.

It's an interesting paradox that embodies most of life's higher truths. If you want love and respect, you need to give it away. If you want to effectively and authentically lead others, you must first learn how to serve them.

When you do, people freely give you authority. You don't have to make demands based upon your title. It evolves from your relationship. When you serve and lead in genuine humility, people follow you out of respect and honor.

INSIGHT - Write the qualities you need to possess to demonstrate authority through a spirit of humility. Seek out opportunities to practice them today.

Use your positional authority to become a servant leader to someone you wish to influence. Create a list of things you can do to help them become more successful.

When you exercise leadership from a spirit of humility, you use authentic relationship, and not authoritative position, to influence. You become a servant leader rather than a servant master. You model and mentor attitudes and behaviors that create a culture of respect and esteem where people feel safe to expand their talents and where honoring one another is seen as a strength not a weakness.

That requires trail blazing leadership. So tomorrow we'll look at steps you can take to put influential leadership to work.

DAY TWENTY

Leading with Purpose on Purpose

STORY - In 1946, psychologist Dr. Victor Frankl published *Man's Search for Meaning*. It chronicled his internment as a Nazi prisoner in Auschwitz during WWII.

He stated that the way a prisoner viewed his future often affected his ability to survive. If he could positively fixate on a purpose for living, visualizing that outcome vividly in the mind, hope could keep him alive. That held true whether the objective was to reunite with family or exact revenge on the Nazis. It wasn't so much the nobleness of intention but more nearly the passion behind the purpose that fueled perseverance amidst persecution.

Purpose *in* life is essential *for* life. The ancient Proverbs tell us, "without a vision, the people perish." Numerous studies have confirmed that truth.

One study of 6,000 people over a 14-year period, reported that those having a sense of purpose had a 15% less risk of death compared to those who didn't.

Infusing purpose into the workplace is also essential to the vitality and productivity of the organization. When there's alignment between the individual's purpose, their functional task, and the organization's purpose, loyalty and performance thrive.

CONCEPT - As a leader, you can't force another's values or reason for being. But you can create discussions for open dialogue and allow others to express how their personal purpose fits into the organization's objectives.

Do they know the mission, vision and values you stand for? Can they plainly articulate what they are? Do they clearly see how their tasks affect the group and the organization's end results?

The stronger these connections are made, and the more you walk the talk of your personal and organizational missions, the better you'll be at influencing others to align with and embrace the vision.

INSIGHT - Write out a brief personal purpose statement for yourself.

Where does it align with your organization's mission and the tasks you perform? Where is it misaligned?

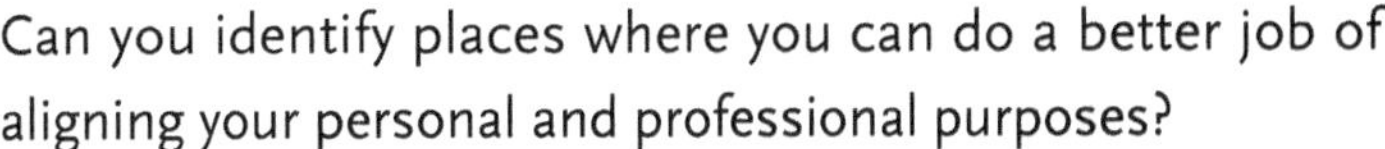

Can you identify places where you can do a better job of aligning your personal and professional purposes?

Create dialogue today to share your purpose and ask others to do the same. Be brave. Ask for one suggestion to help you get better at walking your talk?

Leading with purpose on purpose is the first toolset for the influential leader. Being intentional, each day, to reinforce vision through a message, actions, questions, and open dialogue connects people to their future, creates possibility thinking, and helps people feel contributory toward the world around them. In turn, this will stimulate greater responsibility in their work and stronger accountability toward goals and objectives.

With purpose and vision in place, your next step is to provide a systematic approach to help others get there. Tomorrow we'll see how.

DAY TWENTY-ONE

Framing Your Day for Influence

STORY - Ryan ran a very successful sales team that consistently outperformed other peer groups. He personally invested in each of his team members. He knew their personal values and professional goals, and he'd ask each member what he could do to help them succeed that day. His servant leadership won the trust of his team, so they eagerly followed when Ryan would expand the vision and set expectations for next-level performance.

When asked about his secret for getting higher sales with greater volume, he said, "It's all about how you frame your day."

CONCEPT - Ryan created a strategy for success and taught his team to do the same. Each night he'd prepare by imaging how he wanted the next day to go. Necessary documents were placed and ordered on his desk and phone numbers were laid out. He time-blocked his schedule with priorities set.

Each morning Ryan connected with each team member to communicate vision, purpose, and goals. Next, he chose three high priority clients to contact or send helpful information, and he made 5-10 calls to first-tier prospective clients.

He handwrote three cards each day to follow up conversations and meetings, rather than send email. And he always asked others what he could do to help. He made connections, gave referrals, built bridges, and earned new contacts. He scheduled two times in his day to check emails and return calls. Ryan created a system where he and his team were proactive, efficient, and provided genuine value to others.

INSIGHT -How do you frame your day? Do you intentionally control your schedule, or does your schedule tend to control you?

Begin today to plan with tomorrow in your mind. Use your phone or computer to time-block your schedule and then commit to it. Jot down what people you want to make your priority tomorrow and for the rest of this week.

Who do you wish to connect with personally? Who will you intentionally seek out and offer to help?

Ryans success resulted from an attitude that he grows as others grow around him, along with having a system that helped him manage his day, rather than have his day manage him.

When those you seek to influence see that you are caring and in control and when you take time to share your success strategies with them, you raise the level of efficacy and performance all around you. Do this on a consistent basis and watch your influence grow!

Tomorrow we'll look at handling the challenges that are sure to arise.

DAY TWENTY-TWO

Learning to Navigate Rough Waters

STORY - – Most individuals and organizations do everything possible to avoid adversity. It's rarely fun to encounter roadblocks and challenges. But perhaps the lesson of the steelhead trout can help you influence others to better navigate difficult waters ahead.

Steelhead trout are hatched in the calm of fresh river waters. As they mature, they travel downstream toward the ocean and go through a smoltification process that allows them to safely transition from freshwaters to the salt waters of the sea.

They spawn several times, with just months between each production. But they return to their original hatching grounds to spawn. That means the steelhead trout must make several trips back and forth between freshwater and saltwater. In order to produce, they must learn to swim upstream, travelling paths that run against stiff currents.

CONCEPT - The genius of the steelhead trout develops in the adversity of an upstream environment! It's where their uniqueness, strengths, and persistence come alive.

Confidence in our own capabilities, along with those of others and the world around us, is never certain until we get to test it. Like a muscle, it doesn't grow unless force is exercised upon it.

Conflict and barriers can become opportunities for our strengths, tenacity and creativity to shine. You can lower expectations during challenges, placing yourself "under the circumstances," or you can help others learn to live above them.

Your leadership influence is the sum of your intelligence quotient, emotional quotient, and adversity quotient. Your IQ, EQ, and AQ can help others see their own genius or merely hunker down and give in to the rough roads ahead.

INSIGHT - Think about some of the upcoming changes, challenges, or conflicts you and your people are forecasting. Perhaps you're going through one now. How can you model and mentor the lesson of the steelhead trout so others see the strength and positivity possible in the upstream currents?

When I was going through my first diagnosis of breast cancer, I sought the advice of Diane Tice, a woman I greatly admired for her spirit of intent and her own victory over terminal cancer. Her motto struck deep in my heart and became bedrock for me. She said, "This temporary roadblock will only give you longer legs for bigger strides."

Many times, I've repeated that message and shared it with others going through deep hardship. Tomorrow I share a proven tool for building perseverance in your people.

DAY TWENTY-THREE

Battle-Tested Influence

STORY - There's an Indian Proverb which says, "Tell me a fact and I'll learn. Tell me a truth and I'll believe. Tell me a story, and it will live in my heart forever."

In many ancient cultures, battle victories, miraculous moments or occasions of struggle and overcoming were flagged by placing a stone at the site. These first monuments were used to memorialize the story for generations to come.

The ancients believed there was real power in testimony to shape identity in the people, build faith, and create courage of heart. As they prepared for an upcoming challenge, they used their struggles of the past to rally for the future by declaring, "If we did it before, we can do it again." "If it happened for them, it can happen for us."

Remembering can create the proper perspective that helps people run right into situations that others flee from. Testimony builds boldness to change the circumstances rather than allowing the circumstances to change us.

CONCEPT - When used correctly, our stories have the potential to build resiliency, perseverance, and life-transforming power.

Our past challenges can form in us the expectation of a victim or a victor; they can shape attitudes of cowards or conquerors.

I've used my own testimony of miraculous healing over "incurable" stage 4 cancer with metastases to the bone – without chemo or radiation – as a powerful witness for others. I'm often sought out around the country, and even as far away as New Zealand because I have battle-tested influence that can become the victory cry for others – "If it happened for her, it can happen for me."

Your influence is far more motivating and mobilizing when you share the struggles that built faith, hope, tenacity and perseverance in your own life. When you simply lead from your successes you miss the monumental opportunity to use the power of testimony to build positive expectancy for the future.

INSIGHT - Write down 7-9 major challenges you've experienced in your lifetime. Don't focus on the struggles of the event; rather, go back over each and remember how you came through to the other side.

Next to each event, write the emotion you experienced as a result of overcoming that situation. Perhaps it was peace or courage or gratitude or strength or more.

Once you've identified the challenge and the overcoming emotion, allow yourself to vividly feel the emotions associated with each. Revisit this list regularly when struggles surface and watch your tenacity grow. Use this same exercise to help those you lead.

We tend to connect more with others out of their pain and difficulties than we do their successes. When I'm training leaders, I have them find stories of their own struggle to use as teaching moments, particularly when a storm is brewing.

People don't need cheerleaders in times of uncertainty. They want proven leaders who have experienced the war and lived to tell. That's far more inspiring than the "golden boy or girl" that no one or nothing can touch.

DAY TWENTY-FOUR

THE LANGUAGE OF INFLUENTIAL LEADERS

STORY - I worked with an organization who wanted to improve mindsets around employee safety. While work-shopping various human behavior principles, one associate had a major AHA moment.

Though company goals, mottos, and directives all ostensibly taught safety, they were, in fact, leading employees toward the opposite end result. During new employee training sessions, leaders were giving these fresh, eager, and anxious minds another picture by declaring the "truth" about industry and company standards – "accidents typically happen within the first 90 days!"

Why is this so significant? The mind thinks in pictures. The words you give it create images in your head. For instance, say the word "blue" out loud. What picture emerges? The sky? Water? A room in your house? Or maybe your favorite sweater?

In fact, we teach young children to read by associating symbols arranged in a particular grouping to form a word that's learned with an accompanying picture or some other sensory association like smell, sound, touch or taste. The arranged letters have no meaning apart from the picture we relate to it.

These words – whether it's internal dialogue in your mind or communication you voice out loud – are known as self-talk. Your self-talk is tied to your physiology. It causes you to move toward your target - the most dominant picture you hold in your mind - even if that's not your optimal outcome....even if it proves to be hurtful or harmful to you.

CONCEPT - Self-talk is one of the most powerful tools of an influential leader. Research indicates that you and I have approximately 70,000 thoughts that pass through our mind each day. Most of these thoughts are subconscious and go unchecked, yet they shape our perspectives and perceptions of the world around us.

When our self-talk is negative and self-limiting, we stifle our potential and stunt our growth. When our thoughts are positive and constructive, we envision possibilities that open our awareness to more.

Are your thoughts shaping mindsets fixed on the desired end result, or are you fixating on the current state of affairs?

If you keep saying what you have, you'll keep having what you say.

INSIGHT - Use today to become more consciously aware of your self-talk – both your internal thoughts, as well as what you speak aloud to others. Practice the discipline of "pause" before you speak so you can make space to take every thought captive and examine your words, intentions and the pictures they create in your mind.

Where, when, or with whom do you find your self-talk tending to reinforce the problem? In what circumstances or surroundings do you find you trend more toward speaking in ways that release the potential? Once you become more aware and effective at managing your own self-talk, you can lead others do the same.

To become an effective, influential leader, you must help others envision and speak the solutions rather than ruminate on the problems. "The game is won." "The clients are acquired." "I am healthy and whole."

You don't wait for success to speak success. You create and reiterate the internal picture of success in your mind, first, with strong emotion, and you'll draw yourself and others toward the picture you desire.

That doesn't mean you lower expectations or ignore issues of poor performance. So tomorrow we'll discuss constructive ways to correct others.

DAY TWENTY-FIVE

Fess It and Fix It Leadership

STORY - The Blue Angels are the U.S. Navy and Marines flight demonstration squadron. They first formed in 1946 and are the second oldest flying aerobatic team in the world.

During their amazing air shows, wing spans are a mere eighteen inches apart from one another during their Diamond 360 maneuver. Focus is mission critical! The slightest miscalculation will cause planes and pilots careening to their death.

After each show, they conduct a formal, "after action review" with the team. The process is one of intent. In turn, the pilot begins by acknowledging his gratitude for being a contributing member of the team and safely completing the mission. Next, he reiterates each step of his course, detailing thoughts and actions he made, as well as what he can do better the next time.

This "confess it and fix it" mentality builds the bond of trust within the team; it makes members accountable, self-correcting and solution oriented; and it reinforces expectations for continuous improvement for the next time they perform.

CONCEPT- The "after-action" behaviors of the Blue Angels are consistent with all high performing teams and influential leaders:

- Feedback is immediate and routine...an integral part of each mission. They don't allow time for negativity, judgment, or discord to fester. That allows them to maintain a disciplined and consistent environment of excellence and trust.
- Members have such a clear sense of personal mission for the wellness of the whole team, and they accept the consequences when their individual performance is off the mark.
- By reviewing and taking personal accountability for the past, they move into the future with a sense of responsibility and a clean slate that looks for solutions and sets expectations at a higher level.

INSIGHT - What system or method do you use to correct others in an effective, positive manner – either personally or in a team context?

Refer to the Blue Angels' model. What lessons or tactics can you implement with your group to create a higher standard of accountability and excellence in the people you lead?

Describe in detail how you envision that feedback taking place and the outcomes you desire from it. Create your model; communicate it; then work it consistently with others.

I'm always surprised to learn how few leaders conduct regular after-action reviews.

Many individuals only get feedback annually or when things go wrong. Or perhaps it's not much more than a casual comment in the hallway. When meetings do occur, they're more like status reports, highlighting shortfalls and casting blame on others.

So in the next few messages, we'll focus on how to mentor and monitor your level of excellence to those around you.

DAY TWENTY-SIX

Adjusting Your Focus

STORY - I was working with an automotive dealership to raise the bar on leadership development and store performance. They had nineteen locations, fifteen general managers, and the senior leadership all working toward this effort.

Though the GM's were extremely knowledgeable in their expertise – the car business – it became clear that many had not been formally trained in management skills. Like so many managers, they rose up through the ranks and now managed others like they once had been managed themselves. They were very competitive, demanded a lot, and worked long, hard hours.

When leadership and GM's gathered each month for management meetings, the stress and tension were palpable. Projections and shortfalls dominated the conversation. The negative focus created a heightened sense of urgency that GM's took back and then dumped on the people in their own stores.

CONCEPT- They had developed a punitive cycle of fault-finding vs solution-seeking that stifled quality and innovation.

As they learned the dynamics of culture, motivation, and mindset, they realized the best way to nurture and multiply excellence is to create an atmosphere where they keep their eyes open to what's going right.

They even changed the order and tenor of their meetings by beginning each store report with all the quantitative and qualitative "wins" that were taking place. They celebrated their successes; shared best practices, and left with fresh ideas and energy to take back to their stores.

They modeled this same approach in own store meetings and soon found they could achieve more while pushing, arguing and blaming less.

INSIGHT - Today, pay close attention to your thoughts and words. Which filters through more – the positive or the negative?

Purposefully start today's conversations, meetings, and dinner-time discussions with what's right, what's going well, and what we can look forward to tomorrow. Then watch the atmosphere shift from protective thinking to possibility thinking.

As children, we often got more attention for what we shouldn't be doing than for what we were doing right. And while authority figures tried to keep us safe or well-behaved, we were conditioned to focus on faults and failures.

If we're not consciously aware, we can take that childhood monitoring into our adult managing and create stress-filled, confrontational environments that focus solely on results without how we achieve them.

So tomorrow we'll examine the journey of excellence.

DAY TWENTY-SEVEN

MULTIPLYING EXCELLENCE

STORY - I was on the Pennsylvania Turnpike, traveling to Philadelphia to work with a client, when I came alongside a truck cab without an attached load. It was a clean, yet small and older cab without the markings or logos of a commercial company rig. This was an independent trucker, and I imagined he was deadheading home after a long haul.

What struck me was a modest, yet poignant, sign painted across the back of the cab. In fact, if he had been hauling a load, the height of the truck bed would likely have blocked visibility of the sign. Nonetheless, above the back window of his cab read the words, "Destination Excellence."

CONCEPT - I was captivated. I loved how he used "Excellence" as a physical location, like Destination Disney or Destination Vegas. Here was a guy who was constantly on his way to somewhere, yet the target was always the same...excellence.

As a professional who teaches organizational leaders how to create cultures of excellence, I was impacted and impressed with the passion and purpose of this mobile entrepreneur. And to be honest, I was humbled by my own short-sightedness that this truck driver was more committed to an intentional standard of peak performance than many of the individuals I encounter in most organizations.

He wasn't a guy simply sporting the company slogan. This was an independent driver who chose to live by an ethos that shaped his worldview and drove his behaviors.

INSIGHT - As an influential leader, how do you demonstrate to others your own personal ethos of excellence?

In what activities or circumstances is your excellence best seen by others?

Today - choose a new area to focus your best efforts so you can expand your excellence zone.

When you embrace an ethos of excellence, you understand that it's a continual journey not a final resting place. The minute you think you've arrived, you're lost.

That's because excellence is wrapped up in the essence of continuous improvement where each result invites us to raise the bar. It's the outward pursuit of the inward condition of our spirit that longs for connection with the ultimate and eternal.

So tomorrow I'll give you a leadership tool to help others join the journey.

DAY TWENTY-EIGHT

Multiplying Excellence in Others

STORY - One of the most inspirational leaders and finest mentors I've ever had the privilege of knowing is Dr. James Jackson, founder and chairman of Project C.U.R.E. He built one of the top international medical relief organizations through modeling and mentoring the spirit of volunteerism.

As a non-paid volunteer, Dr. Jackson has amassed donated warehouses, medical supplies and equipment, hundreds of laborers, and even office supplies and furniture by moving the hearts of others. It's a philosophy that's enabled Project C.U.R.E. to grow and impact over 130+ developing countries on less than four percent administrative overhead – unheard of in business and nonprofit operations!

CONCEPT - Jim Jackson is a Level Three-Level Four leader who instinctively multiplies excellence in others. That's what attracts people to him. As his Vice President of Development, I was a direct benefactor of his leadership intelligence and impressive influence zone.

Jim traveled abroad three-quarters of the year visiting developing countries, meeting with country leaders and performing medical needs assessments. But when he was state-side, dignitaries of various types visited our Denver headquarters. Jim always made a point of bringing each guest by my office where he would introduce *them* to *me*. Rather than esteem their title and my privilege to meet them, Jim turned it around. He'd brag on my gifts and accomplishments, and then casually move on to his meeting.

I'd return to my desk feeling two feet taller, smiling in my heart, and ready to conquer the world.

Jim used a subtle yet brilliant method to raise the efficacy of people around him. Instead of complimenting me directly, which I likely would have dismissed as flattery, he used a third party to affirm my strengths and contributions. Whether he was aware or not, this method of sincerely praising the attributes of a person to others around them is an effective and authentic leadership trait that builds confidence, trust, and performance in your people.

INSIGHT - Create scenarios where you can practice this third-party affirmation method. Perhaps it's through an email to an influential person with the recipient cc'd.

Perhaps you compliment your child's behavior to your spouse, making sure your child is within earshot.

Perhaps you begin each meeting by selecting one associate you can praise to the group for a specific action or behavior.

Be creative and consistent. Incorporate this practice into your daily leadership activities and watch collective performance soar to new heights.

A meaningful mentor is one who sees you for what you have the capability of becoming, rather than by where you are. They see more in you than you presently see in yourself.

You can communicate these compliments directly to another; but when you celebrate them through a third party, your words have added weigh and credibility. People are far less apt to deflect the esteem and efficacy you wish to gift them.

DAY TWENTY-NINE

CELEBRATING SUCCESS BY INTENT

STORY - Throughout this process we've looked at how your personality, your past conditioning, your physiology, or health and well-being, and your understanding of others all impact your emotions, motivations, attitudes, and abilities to influence others.

Some people automatically wake each morning full of sunshine and optimism. They abound in energy and cheerfulness. I tend to keep things low and slow, waiting for that cup of coffee to kick in. I've worked hard to retrain my brain to focus on an attitude of gratitude. In fact, I keep a Blessings Book by my bedside where I start the day by writing five things for which I'm grateful. I do this to shift my perspective in the direction of looking for what's right in my world rather than focusing on aches and pains, a restless night's sleep, or the mountain of tasks that lay ahead.

I help organizations do the same. As part of their growth processes, I have them include "Celebrating Success by Intent" into their action plans.

CONCEPT - Most organizations churn and burn through projects and miss the benefits that celebration has for pausing to appreciate contribution, build group efficacy, enhance cooperation, stimulate endorphins, renew energy, and engage in a culture of positive reciprocity.

When you exhibit gratitude and thankfulness, it expands awareness for more. You acknowledge and honor work that's been done, but you create a future expectation and obligation for continued performance. People begin to turn tasks from a "have to" attitude to a "want to, get to, like it, love it," mentality because the rewards are worth the effort.

INSIGHT - As you come to the end of this 30-day journal, consider beginning your own Blessings Book. Start each day with five things you're looking forward to. End the day reflecting and writing on five things for which you were grateful. Do this consistently and watch your heart and relationships flourish in meaningful and measureable ways.

There's nothing more de-motivating than to feel that enough is never enough. Even our organizational competitions run the risk of isolating one winner at the expense of the efforts of all.

Individuals and organizations that practice gratitude through the celebration of success create a community where possibility, creativity, innovation, and inspiration are simply the norm.

DAY THIRTY

Leaving Your Legacy of Influence

STORY - Influence happens, either by intent or neglect. You can't live and move and have your being on this planet without creating impact and influence upon this world. The interdependency of life itself means that even your intake of oxygen and outflow of CO_2 influences the things around you.

Influence can create unthinkable events like the extinction of six million Jews, or it can birth a nation of sacrifice for freedom, faith, and opportunity.

It's your spirit of intent that will dictate whether your influence is self-seeking and self-serving or whether your imprint creates life-producing impact because you were here.

CONCEPT - To what lengths and to what ends your influence zone reaches can be characterized this way:

Sow a thought; reap an act.

Sow an act; reap a habit.

Sow a habit; reap a lifestyle.

Sow a lifestyle; reap a destiny.

What legacy will your destiny hold?

INSIGHT - As a speaker, consultant, and author, I deliver messages of hope, faith, change, possibility, and potential. I often have people offer accolades for my work; for the inspiration it's given them; and how I've helped change their life. I feel blessed and grateful for the significant opportunity to reach the world.

But I'm held in check by an affirmation I once wrote to guide my attitudes and actions toward the ones I love: "I respond in all things in ways that cause those who know me most to like me best."

I certainly fail at it several times a day, but it helps me strive to be a hero in my own home.

If you were to mentor others in one or two lessons from this 30-day process that had the biggest impact on you, what would they be?

What insights did you gain about yourself?

What changes have you made as a result? And how are those changes showing up in others?

It has been my deepest honor and privilege to spend thirty days with you. My hope is that my words, intentions, stories, experiences, and expertise have had meaningful influence on your life and leadership.

As you keep the ideals of purpose, abundance, multiplying excellence, and spirit-driven leadership forefront in your awareness, not only will you expand your vision and enlarge your territory, but you'll find they're filled with champions you've influenced who are ready to raise your cause.

WELL DONE

Congratulations on completing your 30-day journey into

The Influence Zone!

Doreen Lecheler

Maximizing Personal Growth, Influential Leadership Behaviors, and Cultures of Continuous Improvement

Doreen is a capacity-builder, goal-setting expert, international speaker, and best-selling author. Best of all, she's an "incurable" cancer conqueror who gets to live her passion and purpose - growing people and transforming cultures. Whether working with leaders of a nation, community, organization or team, Doreen's work turns meaningful potential into measurable performance by unfolding the process for how to manage your mind.

Doreen began her career in the mid-1980s, helping to progress several start-up nonprofits into regionally, nationally, and internationally recognized organizations. She held senior leadership positions overseeing growth in program development, business development, and organizational advancement.

Since 2000, Doreen has consulted in business, government, education, nonprofits, and athletics, using researched-based tools and techniques for transformation and sustainable goal achievement. Doreen has facilitated high-performance results in the areas of building cultures of excellence, leadership, and team development, change management, employee engagement, goal setting, and vision building. She is a certified speaker for the CEO group, Vistage International.

Doreen has authored two books on personal and professional development. *Growing from Potential to Performance* and *The Influence Zone: Leadership Intelligence that Ignites Results* each provide 30-days of inspiration, learning lessons, and reflection activities designed to upgrade the level of thinking, behavior, and meaningful, measurable results.

Doreen's ability to guide outstanding personal achievement never became more critical than in 2009 with a cancer recurrence staged as "incurable" with metastases to the bone. Aligning life-producing principles of body, mind, and spirit, Doreen experienced miraculous healing with no metastatic evidence of cancer. She fervently shares her cancer-conquering strategies to help others overcome challenges and roadblocks that inhibit well-being and success. She is the author of two books on faith and healing. Her last work, *The Mind to Heal*, was an immediate Amazon inspirational bestseller. She is also the creator of the spiritual growth program, *Destiny Living: Receiving God's Heart for Your Purpose-Filled Potential*.

Doreen has been a Senior Consultant with The Pacific Institute and Excellent Cultures. She holds a degree in Business from the University of Maryland and a master's degree in Theology/ Counseling from Wesley Theological Seminary.

www.DoreenLecheler.com

www.DoreenLecheler.com

Growing from Potential to Performance

Creating transformation by the renewing of your mind

30 Days to Successful, Sustainable Change

GROWING FROM
POTENTIAL TO PERFORMANCE

Creating Transformation by the Renewing of Your Mind

Doreen M. Lecheler

Unleashing potential requires more than a list of steps to follow or attributes to obtain. Real, meaningful, and sustainable change requires an inside-out transformation through the renewing of your mind.

People who experience significant change and higher performance don't succeed because they have more energy, smarts, or will-power; they succeed because they're effective at managing the way they think.

Growing from Potential to Performance gives you knowledge, tools, and insights into how your mind works so you can be more effective at propelling your performance. Using deeply transformative stories combined with neurocognitive research and techniques, along with personal reflection activities, you'll acquire the necessary elements to release higher levels of potential for the life you were destined to live.

www.DoreenLecheler.com

More titles by Doreen Lecheler

For over 30 years Doreen has helped individuals and organizations turn potential into performance, not realizing that one day she'd be using these methods in the fight for her life. She is a stage four, breast cancer conqueror.

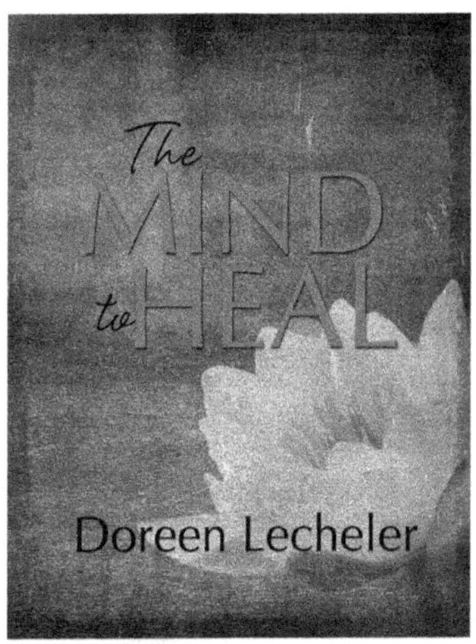

The Spirit to Heal

When Doreen was diagnosed with a breast cancer recurrence in 2009, she wasn't prepared to hear that it was now "incurable," stage four, with metastases to the bone. One prominent institution gave her one year before the metastases would be throughout her body.

As a peak-performance consultant and goal-setting expert, Doreen knew she needed a target. As a faithful Christian, she didn't know which target was meant for her. In her first book, Doreen discovers the truth of what to think in the midst of disease. It is her journey of discovery and faith in the God who seeks to save.

The Mind to Heal

Amazon #1 Inspirational Hot New Releases
Amazon #2 Inspirational Best-Seller

Doreen combines the power of faith with the neurocognitive science of goal-setting and effective thinking skills in this powerful book. Using her own cancer experience, Doreen prescribes seven critical choices necessary to create an environment for healing, health, and wellness. THE MIND to HEAL focuses on how to think in the midst of disease.

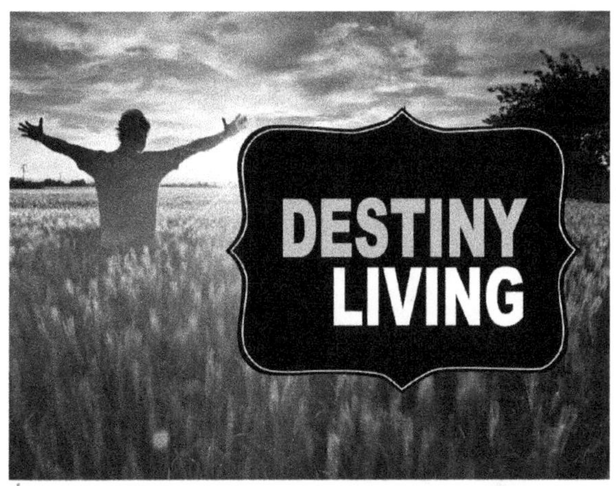

Receiving God's Heart For Your Purpose-Filled Potential

In **DESTINY LIVING**, Doreen brings research from performance psychology, along with biblical principles from God's heart to us, to overcome obstacles and create steps for purpose-filled living. She combines the psychology of break-through thinking with the transformational power of identity and inheritance to create change that is both successful and significant.

For individuals or small groups, **DESTINY LIVING** is a twelve-unit, self-paced program with reflection activities at the end of each unit. The program promotes self-discovery and group dialogue to create engagement with the information and reinforcement of the learning concepts.

12-unit audio program or DVD series, including
Destiny Living workbook

www.DestinyMakers.org
Office@DestinyMakers.org

www.ingramcontent.com/pod-product-compliance
Lightning Source LLC
Chambersburg PA
CBHW052206270326
41931CB00011B/2237

* 9 7 8 1 7 3 3 6 9 0 2 2 5 *